TARA

TARA

by
June Coover

1stBooks – rev. 12/5/00

About the Book

Terrified new parents, Kimberly and Eric, encounter foul play from genius, evil and deceptive doctors, Corona and Mecht. They then come into contact with the police and detectives Borges and Reiber. This nightmare leads to murder along the way; all while Kimberly and Eric strive for justice for their family.

Dedication

Thanks to my parents, Helen and Carl Kugler, now both deceased, for always believing in me and teaching me to never give up and always finish what you started. And to my husband, Donald, who is always my cheering section and believes in my talent. To my grown children, Don Jr., Lavennia, Raebecca and Dale, for being self-reliant and the sensitivity. To Kathy Bliven for encouragement and expectation. To Marian Kline for inspiration and compose.

Chapter 1

The Delivery

What was I doing here? thought Kimberly Shaw. I knew that it just wasn't the right due time. The pregnancy had not taken full term. So what was all this excitement to get me down to Mercy General anyway?

Kimberly kept thinking to herself, What if they didn't notify Eric? He might just be out of town by now! Honestly! You would think the girls at work would have taken my stomach pains a little more lightly. They all have babies at home. Carla just had...to call...my doctor and tell him my symptoms! Of course!, Doctor Corona wasn't at his office.

He was on call for emergencies at the hospital today. Carla also could not stay with me in the outpatient ward. So here I'm all alone! I really do have better things to do. Even if it is to go home and finish the laundry. Whoa! I just don't understand what all these pains are for! I cannot believe they are labor pains because I've got months to go yet!

"Doctor Corona! Doctor Corona! Please come to the outpatient ward," said the nurse on the intercom.

Sounds like he will be here anytime now, raced through Kimberly's mind. Hope that there is really nothing seriously wrong with me. It probably was just that spicy burrito that I had for lunch in the cafeteria. Carla warned me not to eat such a disgusting looking thing. It had probably been there since yesterday or the day before that. Next time I will listen.

"Hope you haven't been waiting too long Kimberly?," said Doctor Corona. "Seems like today everytime I turn around there is an emergency! Usually on Tuesdays it goes pretty slow. Well, let enough alone, let's get onto what is bothering you. If you would kindly step into the examining room and get up on the examining table, I will be right with you. I just need to go wash my hands."

Well, getting up on the table was something else, the pains were so bad by now all I could do was double up with pain. When Doctor Corona came in he hurried and called for the nurse.

"Kimberly, I want you to take a few deep breaths and then I want you to lie down on the table so I can examine the baby. I want to see if it is doing fine. Nurse Low will be here shortly and we will go from there," said Doctor Corona.

"The pain is getting unbearable Doctor Corona! Can't you give me something for it?," yelled Kimberly. "You don't think that the baby is going to arrive early do you? It just can't be! I don't have anything ready and Eric, Eric isn't even here! Why hadn't someone tried to get hold of my husband! Eeeee.....Eeeeee.....! The pain, I can't stand it any longer! Please help me!"

Just then Nurse Low came in and gave Kimberly a shot in the arm. Doctor Corona checked the baby and said to Nurse Low to get her ready for O.B. As she was almost to abandon any hope for pain relief, an arm came out of nowhere and gave her such a big hug.

"Eric, how did you get here?," said Kimberly excitedly. "I was afraid that nobody could get in touch with you. I was also scared because I thought that you might have been called out of town. Eric, I'm so glad that you are here! I'm so frightened and scared that something has gone wrong with the baby. I need to know."

Soon the nurse came back and asked Eric to leave the room a little while until they got the patient ready for delivery. She was in stage four and not much more to go now, they told the young parents to be. This was their first baby and Kimberly thought she knew most everything about the delivery, but she didn't. Eric had tried to attend the baby classes with her, but he was so busy with his job.

Nurse Low got Kimberly into the gown, the one with, the back view. Eric was by her side now. They even had a gown on him, but he was covered! Doctor Corona was all smiles. Kimberly figured that he didn't want to upset her. Kimberly looked at Eric to see if he was upset and how he was handling all this. He looked cool. Kimberly hoped that he could take all this.

"Just push, Kimberly, now when you get a pain again. Eric will hold your head up a little and help you to take deep breaths with each pain. Everything is going to be just fine! Seems as if baby wants to come out and see the world early. 0.K.?, Kimberly, now push, a good one. Do it again, that was a good one, I can see its head. Eric can you see all this in the mirror? Good! Come on Kimberly just a little bit more and push. Push with this next pain, and baby is almost here. I guessed right all the time, a little boy. Congratulations to the both of you! Now I need to stitch Kimberly up a little, while Nurse Low weighs your little son. Hhmmm, six pounds and two ounces not bad for an early bird. Well, got the stitches in, now I'll see that Nurse Low lets Eric back into the room with you for awhile. I will be back later today to check on you," said Doctor Corona.

Kimberly was thoroughly exhausted by now. The shot that Nurse Low had given her was now making her drowsy. She still did not feel like she had got rid of all the stomach cramps. Maybe these are the afterbirth pains that she had heard so many women at work talk about. Kimberly can see that Eric is getting a little tired too. Maybe we will both take a nap.

Eric had just dosed off no more than minutes by the clock on the wall, When......

"Eeeeeee......Eeeeeee.....," screamed Kimberly, "someone take the pain away! Eric! I know that something is wrong. Deep down inside I know that something is not right! Call for Doctor Corona and Nurse Low!"

Eric jumped straight up from his chair and pushed the emergency button by the bed. Then he ran outside to get the doctor himself.

In came Nurse Low wanting to know what all the commotion was about. I explained in a hurried frenzy that the pains in my stomach were so severe that I felt that I had to push! As soon as that, in came Eric and Doctor Corona.

This time the good doctor had a worried look on his face.

"Nurse Low, do another O.B. check on Kimberly and give her another two cc's. Tell the orderly to bring in the gurney and, Eric, let's get ready for another go round," said Doctor Corona seriously.

"What are you doing to me! I have just had a baby!," screamed Kimberly. "Did I tear my stitches or am I hemorrhaging?"

"No, Kimberly, I just think that we should go and have a look inside your uterus and see what is causing your pain. So let's slide you onto this gurney and get going. Eric, I will need your help in calming down Kimberly," said Doctor Corona soberly.

When we got inside of the delivery room it looked cold and dark and unhappy. I had a feeling that Doctor Corona wasn't telling Eric and me the whole truth here. Even Nurse Low was on edge. I had to lift up my legs for him to examine me and then a pain hit. This was one of the grand daddy of all pains yet! I screamed!

"Kimberly I want you to push on the next pain that you get. It looks as thought there is another baby in there. You must have a double uterus which I did not recognize. I can see the head now. This baby is a lot smaller though, compared to your son. O.K. Kimberly push! Push real hard! One more and that should do it. Good one Kimberly! That did it!, said Doctor Corona. Nurse Low get the respirator ready. Kimberly it's a little girl! We will need to keep a close watch on her though. Her lungs are not fully developed. We need help from God above!"

I didn't know what to think because my mind was in such a state anyway. There she was, so tiny, with dark hair and such fair skin. I felt so helpless. I could see the change in Eric now too. We had to leave her and go into my room now. I was sore and tired. I could not rest, I tossed and turned in bed. We both waited for the report on our little daughter.

By evening Doctor Corona was to make his rounds. So far the little one was doing fine. So was her big brother. Twins! This was so unbelievable. I don't recall any on either side.

Chapter II

The Emergency

Beep......Beep...... Beep! Doctor Corona please come to the nursery!," called a nurse on the intercom.

"Eric please get me into the nursery, for heaven's sake! Our baby, I know that is about our baby!," pleaded Kimberly.

Eric saw a wheelchair in the hallway and helped Kimberly into it. She was frantic! He wheeled her into the nursery unannounced. There was Doctor Corona and Nurse Low and another nurse and doctor that they did not know. They were all standing over our baby girl. Her heart has stopped, but they got it going again. They also got the respirator working again. Plus her heart stopped a second time. This time they did CPR, but it did not work. I clung to Eric in disbelief. They tried again and yet again before her heart got started again. Kimberly and Eric could see it on the monitor.

"That was a close one. We will have to have a nurse in here every fifteen minutes until we can get this thing controlled. I think that she is fine for a while. As you can see she has a good steady heart beat now. Kimberly you shouldn't have gotten out of bed yet. You need your rest. Eric you need to take her back into her room," said Doctor Corona.

"Eric, are you sure we can trust the best care here for our little girl? I have a feeling that Doctor Corona really never wanted us to know about her heart condition in the first place. Please, can't we get out of here, you can call another hospital and a doctor?," Kimberly begged.

"Kimberly, you are overreacting about all of this. I'm sure that Doctor Corona will do the best for our little girl. If it will make you feel better, I will stay in the nursery tonight. I will go to tell the doctor right now. I love you Kimberly!," said Eric.

"Maybe I'm overreacting to this situation. I have never been a mother before, especially of twins. We have always had good health. This is the first real medical emergency we have had in the six years of our marriage. I've got to calm down before I get so bad that they will need to drug me," thought Kimberly to herself.

"Well, Kimberly, how are you feeling? Are you hungry yet?," asked Nurse Low. "The doctor said that a meal would be fine for you, so you won't get run down. I heard that it was just vegetable soup tonight. Should I go on ahead and tell them in the kitchen that you would like some. I could order up a bowl for Eric too for this evening."

"That sounds just fine. I am sure Eric is probably really hungry by now. Would you stop by the nursery on your way out and let him know? Thank you, Nurse Low," said Kimberly.

"Well, that sounds better now. I need to get settled down and get my mind off this distrust I have. It shouldn't be too long before the soup will be ready and Eric will be in to keep me company," thought Kimberly happily.

"Hello, are you Kimberly Shaw?," said the orderly.

"Yes, that is right," said Kimberly. "The soup looks good. I see you also brought in a whole tray for my husband, thank you!"

No sooner had he left, than Eric was there. "She is sleeping and breathing well. The doctor said I can stay in there tonight, if you still want me to," said Eric.

"Let's enjoy this soup right now and then I will decide. Eric, did I make a complete fool of myself today? I only wanted what I thought was right about the baby," said Kimberly.

"No, honey! You were just fine. Being a new mother and all and going through what you have been through, it is all right," said Eric.

The soup was real good, it hit the spot. I was wondering to myself if I should ask Eric to get the wheelchair back in here so I could go to see my babies. I guess I could wait, because they were to bring the boy in for his feeding in about an hour. How I longed to hold him! How I also longed to hold her! I told Eric that if he wanted to stay in the nursery it was his decision. Whatever he decided it would be fine.

I was so tired by now and Eric was too. So we both took a nap. We were awakened by the nurse bringing in our little boy. He was howling! We were laughing at how healthy he was. I didn't want to breast feed and now I had a good reason, not to with two babies. As soon as the nurse gave me the bottle, into his mouth it went. Soon all his wailing had stopped. While I was watching him eat I kept remembering the commercial about the cat food, chow, chow, chow. He reminded me of a kitten for some reason.

Eric asked to hold him after he was fed and burped. I asked him if the little person reminded him of a kitten, but Eric just laughed at the thought. He wanted to know where I get all these crazy ideas. So while he held our little boy, he told me that he had decided to go ahead and sleep in the nursery, at least for tonight. He wanted to be close to his baby girl.

"That will be just fine," said Kimberly. "You can't sneak me in there for tonight or can you?"

"No, I want you to get your rest," said Eric.

The nurse came in to get the baby. Eric then left for the nursery. I told myself I had better do what Eric said and get some rest. Then the nurse came in and was going to give me some medication when.....

"This is strange, I will be right back. I must go and check this out with my supervisor," said the young nurse.

I had seen the alarm in her eyes. Maybe I am just doing that silly thing with my imagination again. Well, no use going to sleep until she gets back.

"Sorry that I took so long, Kimberly," said the young nurse. "I just wanted to make sure that this was right. It was written down so my supervisor O.K.'d it. This should go to work in just a little bit."

"You don't look as though you really want to give this to me," said Kimberly. "Is there something that I should know that you are not telling me? Please?, Please let me know."

"I just think that it is strange that they would want to give you such a high dosage," said the young nurse. This will knock you out until tomorrow morning. I guess the doctor wants you to get your rest. Don't worry, it is not dangerous or anything."

So I consented without making a fuss. It wasn't too long after that, before, I was really getting sleepy! I was out!

"I think I will go in and check Kimberly, nurse. I'll be right back. Do you think that they could spare me a pillow for that chair?", said Eric.

Good she is resting. She looks like an angel. I hope tomorrow will be a lot better for her and me too. Well, now I'll go back into the nursery to be with the rest of my family.

Eric bent down to the bedside and kissed Kimberly tenderly.

"Love you Kimberly!," whispered Eric.

"I see that the nurse got me my pillow. I'm going to go check out the babies. Good, he is fine and her respirator and monitor are doing O.K. I think that I will take a few winks myself."

Chapter III

Dreams

Eric had dosed off for awhile when.....

"Hello there, Mr. Shaw," he heard the young nurse. "Would you like to have some juice or ice or ice cream before you retire? I can bring it now or on my next rounds, which would be in about half an hour."

"Later would be fine. I just finished with supper and I think that I want it to settle. I'll take the strawberry ice cream, please," said Eric.

"Hello, Eric," this time it was Doctor Corona. "I see that you did decide to stay the night in the nursery. I'm very glad to hear that! I hope that Kimberly is taking all this fine. I suppose by tomorrow she will have rested and not be so distraught. Now I will just check these two before I go. Your son is fine and it seems that your daughter's breathing all checks out well; the heartbeat is a little high, but, it is no cause for concern. I'll see everyone tomorrow morning."

"This has been quite a day. I still think I will take a little cat nap before the nurse brings in my ice cream," thought Eric.

"Nurse Low, have you seen Doctor Mecht?," asked Doctor Corona. "He is supposed to stay and make sure the little Shaw baby is monitored well tonight and watch her breathing."

"I haven't seen him yet doctor, but I will let him know as soon as he comes in," said Nurse Low. "He usually isn't this late."

As Kimberly slept she tossed and turned. Her dreams repeated the death of her baby girl. Once the respirator had stopped, the other was the heart monitor stopped. She was so drugged that she could not wake up at all; it was like being in limbo. Being helpless and not being able to help her baby. All she could do in her dreams was stand there while her baby died.

"Are you ready for your strawberry ice cream?, Mr. Shaw? The freezers here aren't as cold as they should be. This is like soft batch ice cream," said the young nurse.

"Thank you, I'm sure that it will be just fine. I needed something to tide me through the night," said Eric.

Eric finished his ice cream, which was more than a little sloppy, before he left the room. He went into Kimberly's room to wash off the stickies. When he came back, he noticed that someone else had been there, because his pillow was on the floor. He had left it flat on the chair seat. Also there was a certain smell, one that he couldn't recognize. He thought surely that they would come back if it was important. He put the pillow back under his neck on the chair and went to sleep.

In his dream he dreamed about someone reaching over the back of his chair and around his head. Then they put something over his mouth and his nose. He heard a scuffle, which he thought was just a dream also, but it sounded like Doctor Corona's voice and he was saying something like this.. "Be sure that you take the respirator away for only a few minutes at fifteen minute intervals. Then after that inject two cc's of Phenacetin. This may induce excessive breakdown of the red blood cells, thus making her eventually brain dead. Then he heard another man's voice. One that he couldn't pinpoint. This man was saying that by morning he would have all this taken care of and the certain party notified. They would deal with the parents in an orderly way.

Kimberly was still having bad dreams. The strange thing is that she kept hearing Doctor Corona's voice and then another voice that she didn't know. They were talking about her baby girl and something about brain damage. That they could keep the rest of the body alive on a machine. In her dream Sanction B&F came up. Something about this had to be kept top secret.

Kimberly and Eric did not know what devious things were being done on their baby girl. What they didn't know was that Doctor Corona hadn't told them the whole truth about the little girl; the last time when her heart had stopped, there was more damage done than expected. This was just what they were looking for at Sanction B&F.

Chapter IV

Tragedy

Beep! Beep! "Nurse get in here!," yelled Doctor Mecht. "Tell Doctor Corona to get down to the nursery. I think the baby's heart has stopped and we need the electrodes. Also go tell Nurse Low to notify the mother to get in here. Her husband must have had quite a night; he is still sleeping through all this!"

Nurse Low went into Kimberly's room to wake her. She thought it odd that she was sleeping so soundly. "Kimberly, dear, wake up, there is an emergency in the nursery with your little girl!," said Nurse Low with a look of seriousness on her face. "I don't know all the details as yet. Let me help you up to the bathroom and I'll then put you in this wheelchair. Does that sound all right to you?"

"Fine! Fine! Let's just hurry," said Kimberly. "I just knew something was going to go wrong. I had such horrid, horrid, nightmares last night! Eric, why isn't Eric in here to help me?"

"He is still asleep, dear," said Nurse Low.

"That is odd because Eric is such a light sleeper; a pin dropping on the floor would wake him!," said Kimberly.

Finally, the nurse got Kimberly into the nursery. They both tried to wake Eric. He finally comes to and wakes up and is just terrified at what he sees. Kimberly is in hysterics too! Two doctors are working with two nurses over their little girl. Eric is still groggy and thinks this is still part of one of his bad dreams. Kimberly reassures him that this is not and is reality.

"You were here all night, Eric! Didn't you know that something was wrong?," yelled Kimberly. "You normally don't sleep like this. Maybe it is because of all the stress and strain."

"I don't know what happened, since I first rested in the chair! She was fine when I had went to sleep!," said Eric. "Who is the other doctor?"

"I don't know!," said Kimberly. "Nurse Low, who is the other doctor with Doctor Corona?"

"He is Doctor Mecht, and he is a new resident doctor here. His qualifications are excellent," said Nurse Low.

"I can't seem to get this little girl to fight back or show the will to live. I don't understand, she was doing so well last night. Doctor Mecht, how was she while you monitored her last night on your rounds?," asked Doctor Corona.

"She was doing beautifully, even her breathing was excellent. I just don't understand. We must have missed something in her diagnosis. Doctor, she can't take much more of this! There she goes, electrodes, stand back! No good! Stand back! Try again, No good. Try again, Stand back, Still nothing!," said Doctor Mecht.

"Her breathing stopped too long; possible brain damage," said Doctor Corona sadly. "I'm sorry Kimberly and Eric, but we tried the best that we could. I would like you to consider under these circumstances that it might be a good idea to have her remains sent to this very reputable institution and have an autopsy performed. That way we would all know what was the cause of her death."

Kimberly is sobbing hysterically and Eric is trying to hold back the tears coming to his eyes. They both look on over to the little boy who is sleeping peaceful through this whole ordeal.

"It is just too soon for us to make a decision, doctor!

Let Kimberly and me discuss this later this afternoon," said Eric.

Kimberly and Eric go on back into Kimberly's room. They are two very unhappy new parents right now.

"Do you want me to put up all this equipment, now? And do you want me to go and get the coroner and the place in the freezer ready in the basement?," asked Nurse Low.

"Not just yet; the doctor and I have a few ends to tie up here, yet. If there are not more emergencies that call us away, Doctor Mecht and I can do all that," said Doctor Corona.

"That is highly irregular, isn't that doctor? Isn't there some other patients that you need to be tending to?," asked Nurse Low.

"Yes, this is indeed irregular, Nurse Low, but we want to make sure that everything is in order in case the parents do consent to have the baby sent to Noitcnas Laboratory. I'm hoping to get done quickly with the help of Doctor Mecht. So I can get back to my other patients," said Doctor Corona.

"I guess it will be all right, but what do I put in the nurse's report doctor?," asked Nurse Low.

"Just put down 'circumstances pending' in the doctor's logo," said Doctor Corona.

"That should suffice for the superiors, doctor. Thank you, and now I'll go and do my rounds for medication," said Nurse Low.

Kimberly and Eric were so grief stricken that they couldn't eat their lunch. Kimberly needed to hold their son for a feeding soon. Eric thought this might calm her down a little. Only as soon as the nurse brought in their son and put him into Kimberly's arms, she sobbed profusely. Eric had to take their baby son and give him his feeding. Eric noticed just how good a baby he was. He had hoped that Kimberly would have noticed that, too. Only he knew she was much to preoccupied with grief.

"How could this have happened Eric? Maybe we should have taken her to a better equipped hospital? Maybe Doctor

Corona really didn't know all the circumstances. And if that was so, then why didn't he tell us the real truth that he didn't know, what really was wrong with her?," said Kimberly sobbingly. "I have a bad feeling about this whole thing, Eric. Maybe it is just my imagination. Or maybe it is just those horrid dreams." Kimberly then tells Eric the details of her dreams.

"What do you think? Do you think that I'm losing my mind? Eric!, Talk to me, don't just give me that overcome look," said Kimberly.

"Kimberly, I don't know what to say to you. One of the main points in our life has left us. Then you tell me about your bad dreams. I had some strange dreams, too. So he proceeded to tell her about his dreams. She was aghast at hearing his! I'm now wondering deep down inside of my conscious if these were dreams or a reality," said Eric.

At this point the nurse came back in to take the baby. They still had not picked out a name for him. The nurse said the office needed it tomorrow for the birth certificate. They also needed a name for the little girl for the death certificate. Kimberly broke down sobbing and said by tomorrow.

Chapter V

Suspicion

In came Doctor Corona and wanted to know what they had decided. They hadn't discussed it yet.

"Could you give us until tomorrow doctor? By then we will have a decision," said Eric.

"Very well Eric; could it be by noon?," asked Doctor Corona.

"I think that will be fine," said Eric.

After that the doctor left.

"Did you see the look on his face when you said not until tomorrow?," said Kimberly. "Usually he is all smiles and gladness. I really don't know if I want her to go through the autopsy. I think I would rather have her rest in peace. We can have a small service for her at that small chapel where we got married. We have to get a small burial lot; well, no, better we get a larger one so we all can be beside her. Does that sound all right with you?"

"Kimberly, if that is what you want it can be that way. Right now though I want you to get some rest. I need to get back to the office before this evening so that Bill can finish out the rest of this week's criteria in order. I love you Kimberly and don't you forget it!," said Eric. And he hugged and kissed her, lovingly.

After Eric left she decided that maybe if she turned on the television for awhile and did relax that she could go to sleep. It wasn't long until she dozed off. She hadn't been asleep too long when she thought she heard voices and shouting. Two men's voices and they were coming from the nursery. She wasn't going to pay much attention to it anyway, because the television blocked out a lot of their words. But, when the word Shaw came up she was curious.

Kimberly tiptoed out of bed; she left the television on hoping that they would think she was still in her room. She checked the hallway, no one was coming. She tiptoed down the hall into the next room to the nursery. No one was in it at the time so she closed the door. She put her ear to the wall and heard the two men's voices distinctly this time. Why! It was the good doctors, Corona and Mecht. They were saying that they had to get the Shaw baby out of here tonight before Nurse Low would suspect anything. They had put the baby in the basement on a respirator, so it would still be a warm tissue specimen. So, when they sent it to the laboratory it would not be stiff and blue.

This made sense to Kimberly, but they still did not have hers nor Eric's consent to take the baby out of the hospital. So, Kimberly went back to her room cautiously and called Eric. It seemed he had gone on an errand with Bill. The secretary told her that he left a message for her and it said he would not see her until seven o'clock.

She knew that feeding time was coming up, so she had better be in the room for that. She would ask the nurse to take the baby early because she was tired. Then, that would give her more than an hour to sneak down into the basement before Eric arrived.

Soon the nurse came in and as usual the little boy was sucking his fingers furiously. He had quite an appetite. In no time, he finished that bottle of formula. She waited fifteen minutes and then rang for the nurse to get him. She explained that she was exhausted and wanted a little shuteye. She didn't want to be disturbed for about an hour. The nurse wrote that on her roster.

Kimberly got up and put on a pair of pajamas. Put on her warmer slippers and headed out into the hallway. Whoops!..... Here comes Doctor Corona. She hurriedly took off her slippers, put them under the bed, and pulled up the sheets and blanket to her neck so he would not notice that she had changed.

"Kimberly I just wanted to see how you were doing before I finished my round. I see on the roster that you do not want to be disturbed for about an hour. I think that is fine and that is why I stopped in now so as not to bother you later. This is my last evening rounds, but I can stop back in about an hour or so when I get done with the other patients. How is your stomach? And how are the stiches? Should I have a look or should I wait until later?," asked Doctor Corona.

"Why don't we wait until later this evening doctor, and I would really like to get some sleep now. I don't mean to be rude; it has been a rough morning for me," said Kimberly.

"That will be fine. Have a good rest," said Doctor Corona.

"Well that wasted about ten minutes. I really don't walk that fast anyway with these stiches. I don't even know just where I go to get down to the basement or when I get down there where I can find her. I'm so scared, I'm talking and answering myself! I've got to get a hold on myself and take some deep breaths. Put my slippers on and prop up my pillow, so they will think that it is me. I think that I will turn it so I will have my back to the door and face down. That should do it. Okay, no one is in the hallway; let her rip, as they say," Kimberly said to herself.

Chapter VI

Proof

Kimberly went down to the end of the east hallway. They are really called corridors, she found out. The sign said take corridor two, north to corridor one, to the elevator. She walked as fast as she could; now her stiches were hurting. She hoped she would not tear any. She had luck so far, no one had seen her. She got into the elevator and pushed basement. The basement was down at least nine floors. She looked at her watch. She was making good time so far. The elevator stopped, the door opened; she only hoped that no one would be down there to see her. No one was there, only a long empty corridor with smaller attached corridors. It was chilly and kind of damp down there.

She walked slowly down the large corridor; it seemed to be going south. A way down she noticed a sign. It read D.O.A.'s, aborted, accidental and unknown. She took the unknown. The sign said to go to corridor four, and turn right into corridor six. That seemed well and simple. She checked her watch again just as she got into corridor six. She was still doing fine, at least timewise.

In corridor six were several rooms and by now she noticed a definite change in the temperature. It really was getting cold. She went past four of the rooms marked unknown, when she saw the name shaw. She was going to enter the room when she heard voices. It was Doctor Corona and Mecht. What were they doing down here? They were supposed to be doing their rounds. She sneaked into the room across the corridor, scurrying as fast as she could, and as noiselessly as she could to crawl under something. She really didn't know what it was because it was so dark.

At least she had a good view of the other room. She was sure that they could not see her. And she could hear their conversation just fine.

"Do you think if I put her into this jar with this respirator that she will be a good specimen? We have never sent one there in four gallon jars. They should be called tubs. It seems as if she is alive!," said Doctor Corona.

"Does this mean that they will still be able to use the brain tissue?," asked Doctor Mecht.

"You did a good job on using the Phenacetin. They should still be able to use the brain tissue. They should pay both of us a lot for this little one," said Doctor Corona.

"I was feeling nauseous now. They were talking about a part of me. My beautiful little baby girl, as a hunk of meat! I saw her in that jar, she did look alive. I thought maybe she still is and that they lied about that. But, I knew, deep down, that wasn't true. Still I didn't want them to have her for, who knows what?," thought Kimberly to herself.

"The time! I can't read my watch. I'm going to have to sneak out of here fast. Just as soon as they turn around again, I will leave. Okay, Kimberly, this is it, go!...... Made it, even if it is into another room. This one is just beside the room that they are in. Maybe if I carefully stretch my arm down near the light I can tell what time it is. Here goes!, Good, I have twenty minutes to get out of here and upstairs and into my bed. Now's the time to go do it again Kimberly, while they are still talking. Great! I'm out of corridor six and into corridor four!," thought Kimberly excitedly.

She got out of there into the larger corridor and she could see the elevator. Wait!....."I hear someone, oh no! It is an orderly and he is bringing down a corpse! Now where do I hide! I guess this will do!," panicked Kimberly.

Kimberly took the nearest room to the west. What she didn't know though was, it was the same room the orderly was going to. The room was dark and she hid under something, something cold, hard, and stiff. She heard the orderly coming and she huddled under whatever it was in a panic. She felt her heart come up to her throat! In came the orderly with the corpse. It was there right beside her now! She held back a scream! Thank goodness he didn't turn on the light! He hung the body on something. She didn't want to know. Soon he left and she got up and looked to see what she was hiding under.

She held her hand over her mouth so hard it was bleeding! She cut her lip on her tooth. She had been hiding under a corpse! She didn't want to know if it was a he or she either. She just wanted out of there! She had to wait for the elevator to get back down, and she was down to twelve minutes! No time to lose! The elevator door opened and in she went. She counted the nine floors under her breath. She was cold and shivering yet! Plus, she had the living daylights scared out of her! The elevator door opened.....the coast was clear. Out the elevator she went and down the corridor that she had been on before and back on the maternity and nursery floor.

She looked around to see if anyone had noticed her, then hurried to put the slippers into the closet, take off her pajamas, throwing them onto the closet floor before closing the door. She then wriggled back into that awful gown, hopped into bed and checked her watch. She had a whole minute to spare! She took a couple of deep breaths as Eric and Doctor Corona walked in!

Chapter VII

More Trouble

"Hello honey, hope you got a good rest! I'm glad to get back here at the hospital with you! I had left a message at the office as you know, saying that I would be late. Aren't you glad that I'm early? I got all the criteria in order earlier than expected. I found out that Bill is a lot more capable of handling these things than I expected," said Eric happily.

"Eric if you don't mind, would you please step out into the corridor until I get done with examining Kimberly? It should just take a couple of minutes. Well Kimberly, let's have a look, oh, oh, what have you been doing, Kimberly? I thought that you were going to rest. There are three stiches that are torn. Were you up and pacing around? I need to call in a nurse to bring in the anethesia and the equipment to replace these three. Just stay on the bed as you are," said Doctor Corona.

Kimberly was so glad that he didn't have any way of knowing where she had been. She saw in his face and his eyes that he just figured that she was overdoing it. She was also glad that it was just three stiches and not anything worse.

"Nurse, would you come into room three? I need the normal for a redo stitch. Also, would you tell Nurse Low that I need to talk with her. Thank you. This shouldn't take too long, Kimberly. See the nurse is here, already. I'll be real gentle with this needle. Now we will wait for that to go to work and we will replace those three. Kimberly, count to thirty out loud. I'll be right back," said Doctor Corona.

While Kimberly was counting she noticed that Nurse Low and Doctor Corona were talking. She couldn't hear a word they were saying. And she didn't see Eric out in the corridor. Maybe he went down to the cafeteria for some coffee. That didn't take long to discuss, as here he comes.

"Okay Kimberly, nurse do you have it threaded? Let's get going then. One, then two, and three. See, that didn't take long. I'll go and find Eric and send him back here with you. I won't be stopping back anymore tonight. I will, though, stop in the nursery and see the baby. Have You named him yet?," asked Doctor Corona.

"No, not yet. Eric and I have until tomorrow noon to discuss a name for both babies," said Kimberly.

"Both babies!, has Nurse Low discussed anything with you as yet?," asked Doctor Corona.

"No she hasn't, what has that got to do with naming my two babies anyway? I need a name for the death certificate," said Kimberly.

"I will send Nurse Low down later this evening after you have fed your little boy. Then if you have any questions after your talk, you can get a hold of me tomorrow," said Doctor Corona.

Chapter VIII

Names

Kimberly did not like the way Doctor Corona said both babies. She also wished that Eric could get back in here soon. She wanted to know just what Nurse Low had said to Doctor Corona. She was hoping that Eric had heard their discussion. And if Eric didn't get back soon she would have to discuss all this after her last evening feeding of the baby.

No sooner than she had thought of that, in came the nurse with the baby. He was quite content tonight it seemed. Doesn't seem as hungry, he was not sucking his little fat fingers. He is so warm and cuddly, and there is that fresh baby smell that lightens ones heart.

"Kimberly, I had gone down to the cafeteria for a cup of coffee and a roll. I got to talking to another dad and we both kind of lost track of the time. He looks so sweet, after you finish feeding and burping, I want to hold him," said Eric.

"I think that can be arranged, since you are his dad. You need to get used to holding him anyway. After he goes back to the nursery, could we have a talk?," asked Kimberly.

"You sound serious, hope nothing is worrying you again? Okay, hand him over to his daddy. How are you champ. Look at those hands, he is going to be a big kid, that is once he does start to grow. He kinda looks a lot like me don't you think? Guess all this is boring him, because he went to sleep. Well, here is great big kiss from daddy. I'll ring for the nurse to come and get you. Mommy and I are going to get in a big discussion now," said Eric.

The nurse came in to take the baby, she asked if they would like a snack later and if so to let her know after they ate supper, about thirty minutes from now.

They said that they would. Kimberly wanted to know if Eric could eat with her again or needed to go down to the cafeteria. The nurse said that it would be better if he got his food in the cafeteria, but he could bring it back to this room. Just make sure to tell the cashier it is to go.

"Thank you, and I will do just that. Now Kimberly, what is so important to discuss. I didn't think to just pick out baby names was such a big deal! Or is there something else on your mind that you need to tell me?," asked Eric.

"First let's get the names out of the way. I have four names picked out for each child. I'll tell them to you and then you can decide. Anyone you pick will be fine because I really do like all of them. For the girl I picked out Heather, Lavennia, Steffanie and Tara. For the boy I picked out Scott, David, Darren and of course Eric Junior. I want you to think seriously about them and then after I get done taking my shower you let me know which ones you chose. I'll try and not be too long," said Kimberly.

"I'll have the two names picked out by the time you get out of the shower, dear. You don't need to hurry I'll still be here. I'm going to watch a little television while I think," said Eric.

Kimberly hoped that Nurse Low would come in soon after they ate. This would help her in discussing a lot of what is going on around here. This shower felt great, a good tension reliever!

Eric pondered the names in his head while watching the news. He distinctly liked Tara for the girl and Eric Junior for the boy. Got one problem solved and out of the way. Looks like not a minute too soon. She just got out of the shower.

"Well, did you decide on a couple. When you do, instead of waiting for tomorrow, would you give them to the nurse at the front desk, so it can be taken care of soon?," asked Kimberly.

"I'll go down there right now. I chose Tara for the girl and Eric Junior for the boy. I'll see you in a little bit, dear. I love You," said Eric.

As he was leaving, in came supper. Kimberly told the nurse that they would like to have a snack later, probably ice cream and any kind would be fine. The chicken didn't look too bad for tonight. Kimberly wondered what Eric would bring back to eat from the cafeteria.

"Well, I see that you are eating; looks good; enjoy. I will go see what is on the menu downstairs in the cafeteria. Be back whenever," said Eric.

Kimberly sat down and ate her food. As she ate she tried to get all the details of today down clearly in her mind. She had to discuss this calmly and directly and urgently with Eric. Still, it had to be after Nurse Low had talked to them and also she needed to find out if Eric had heard anything that Nurse Low and Doctor Corona were discussing.

"Well, it's Salisbury steak tonight. Not too bad; hope it is still warm because I'm starved. The front desk nurse put the names in the files. They will be taken care of early tomorrow morning. Did you want to have that discussion now?," asked Eric.

"Let's wait a little while after we both eat. I would like to enjoy my food and bet that you would too," said Kimberly.

Chapter IX

The Discussion

They were both close to finishing when Nurse Low walked in. She apologized for intruding on their supper, but this was the only time that she could make it for this discussion that Doctor Corona had wanted. She looked at them both and her eyes proceeded taking note.

"Doctor Corona wanted you to wait until the autopsy was completed before they put a name on the tag on the baby. The reason is, that people down at the laboratory get too involved and upset if they have a name. They have so many babies go through that laboratory. They don't want to get attached to each and everyone. It is really heartbreaking they say and they do their best to find out the causes of death, without wondering who Susan or Jeff is or belongs to. The babies are sent with a coded number under their forefinger and are tagged on their foot. Not one number is the same and will be recorded in their computers and in ours. There is no way they can lose your baby. I have seen good work done there and they don't take long," said Nurse Low.

"I'm glad to know all about this Nurse Low. My wife and I will talk it over and let you and Doctor Corona know tomorrow. Thank you for stopping in to see us about this," said Eric.

After Nurse Low left, Kimberly was dumbfounded. Nurse Low actually did not know what was going on here. She trusted Doctor Corona without a doubt and had good reports back also. That means that those people really had gotten their babies back! Kimberly didn't understand.

"Eric did you by chance hear what Nurse Low and Doctor Corona were talking about in the corridor this evening earlier, while you were waiting for my examination. It really is important that I know," said Kimberly.

"I only heard a little of it because then I decided to go down to the cafeteria. They were talking about you and how you could have torn your stitches. Doctor Corona had asked Nurse Low if she had seen you out walking in the corridors or anything. Or if any of the nurses on duty had seen you out and about. By the way did you go out for a walk or just walk around the room a lot?," asked Eric.

"Eric close the door and make sure that no one is coming. If someone should come in while we are talking we will change the subject completely, all right? This afternoon when I was going to take my nap I heard voices and recognized Doctor Corona's but not the other voice right away. I had the television on so a lot of it was blocked out. When I heard the word Shaw mentioned and the talking got louder, I sneaked out to see what it was all about. They were saying that they had to get the Shaw baby out of the hospital tonight. And before Nurse Low would know anything about it. That they have the baby in the basement on a respirator so that it will be a warm, not stiff specimen. I then sneaked back into my room. That is when I called your office and you had left me that message. I knew that feeding time was soon. I would ask the nurse to take the baby early after the feeding. I explained that I was very tired and wanted to not be disturbed for about an hour. The nurse said that she would write that down on the roster," said Kimberly.

"I got up after the nurse left and put on my slippers and pajamas. I headed out into the corridor. But, to my dismay, Doctor corona was coming. I hurried and put my slippers under the bed and pulled the sheet and blanket up to my neck so he would not notice that I had changed. He had noticed on the roster that I wanted to be left alone for awhile. He said that he stopped in so as not to bother me until his evening rounds. He wanted to know if I wanted to be checked now or later. I said later. After he left I put on my slippers and I propped up my pillow so it would look as if I were sleeping sideways with my back to the door," said Kimberly.

"I then sneaked out and went down the corridor to the elevator. I pushed the button that said basement, and held my breath until the door opened. I went down the main corridor until I got to a sign. It read, D.O.A.'s, aborted, accidental and unknown. I took the unknown directions that said to go to corridor four and turn right into corridor six. I went by four rooms marked unknown, no luck. When I got to room five I noticed the name Shaw. I was going to enter the room when I heard voices. It was Doctor Corona and Doctor Mecht. They were supposed to be on their evening rounds. I thought, what were they doing down here?," said Kimberly.

"I sneaked into the next room across the hall. I had a good view of the room and I was sure that they could not see me. It was so dark in the room. It seems that the good doctors want to sell Tara for her brain tissue. Doctor Corona was thanking Doctor Mecht for giving Tara some kind of an injection of, I believe, it was called Phenacetin. Doctor Corona said that they should get paid a lot for her," said Kimberly.

"I was worried about the time and I couldn't read my watch because it was dark, but knowing that I had to get out of there and get back to my room. When they turned around I made my move to the room right beside the one they were in. I put my arm down near the light near the floor shining in from their room. I had a good twenty minutes," said Kimberly.

"I got up and sneaked out into corridor six into corridor four. Got into the main corridor and was heading to the elevator when I saw the elevator light on. I had to hide, and the orderly was coming with a corpse. I hid in the nearest. room. It was dark and cold. I heard the orderly coming, coming into the room that I was in. He put the body right beside me. I held back a scream! Thank goodness that he didn't turn on the light. When he left I got up and looked to see what I had been hiding under and it was a corpse. I put my hand over my mouth so hard so as not to scream that my tooth cut my lip. See, right here," said Kimberly.

"I had to wait for the elevator to get back upstairs and I had about twelve minutes left now which made me worry worse. Got into the elevator and counted the floors under my breath. Hoped no one would see me get off the elevator, or on the main corridor here before I got back into my room. I hurried and changed and got into that awful hospital gown. I had about a minute left and took some deep breaths. Then in walked you and Doctor Corona. One thing that I don't understand is how Nurse Low hasn't found out what Doctor Corona is doing. She really trusts him and thinks this is a great help that he is doing," said Kimberly.

Eric just sat there with anxiety and stupefaction on his face. He knew deep inside his soul that what Kimberly had told him was true. Her lip was cut and her tone of voice wasn't one of a crazy woman. That was probably how she managed to tear her stitches, also. It was too much for anyone to make up.

Chapter X

Check Facts

"Kimberly, I want you to stay in here for awhile. I'm going to go down in the basement and have a look for myself. Now don't worry, I will be careful. I have an hour and a half until visiting hours are over, so they should not get too suspicious. That is, if they don't see me going somewhere. If someone wants to know where I am, say either the cafeteria or the men's room. Stay calm and I will see you in awhile. Love you, Kimberly!," said Eric.

Kimberly knew he believed her and she knew that he would handle everything for her. Eric would not let her baby Tara be taken away for body parts. She also needed to look calm, so she turned on the television.

Eric remembered the way that Kimberly had taken. The hardest part was to get on and off the elevator without being noticed. So far, so good, now that he was in the basement he turned down corridor four and into corridor six. Then he counted to five rooms and there was the name Shaw. It was dark inside so he turned on the light. There was Tara in a large tub of some sort with what looked like a breathing apparatus through her nose. He was going to touch her when he heard voices. He shut off the light and slipped into a closet.

In came Doctors Corona and Mecht. They were trying to decide the best time to dispose of the baby without anyone seeing the van pull up outside the basement door. It would have to be a time when Nurse Low was off duty and a novice nurse was on. They decided on one-thirty in the morning. Then they left.

Eric waited quite awhile in the closet before he came out. He went out into the corridor to make sure they had left and that no one else was coming. He then turned on the light and knew that he had to find a way to save Tara and more babies just like her. They were supposed to put a number of some kind under her forefinger. This had not been done as yet, nor was she tagged with a number. First, before he left he had to make sure of a way that he could identify Tara.

He thought of a place that they would not do scientific research on. It had to be her mouth. Yes! Inside her mouth. Still he thought, what could he put inside her mouth to show that she is my baby. His mind raced around diligently and he finally got a good idea. He went back into the closet and turned on the light and looked to see if he could find any scissors. Luck was on his side because he did find just that.

He then took out his billfold and opened it. He proceeded to take out his credit card, cut out his name laying it down on the table; put back the scissors, shut off the closet light, and closed the door.

Picking up the rest of the credit card, he put it into his billfold and back into his pocket. Then he took the piece that he had cut out over to where Tara was in the tub. He gently lifted her without pulling out the breathing apparatus; pressed hard and squeezed the piece of credit card in between her small lips into her mouth. Then he gently put her back into the tub of liquid. Next he went out into the corridor cautiously.

No one was coming, so he went down corridor six and then back into corridor four and back into the elevator. His heart was pounding now and sweat was beading down his forehead. He hoped that no one was around when he got off the elevator and back into room three.

"I'll close the door! Let me catch my breath and do a little thinking. You were right Kimberly; they want to use our Tara for parts! We cannot stop this alone, you know! No one here at the hospital would believe us. I will need to call the police! What number do I push to call out?," asked Eric.

"Push number seven and then wait for the dial tone. Let me look up the number of the Fifth Precinct. The telephone book is underneath the two drawers in the stand by the bed. Give me a minute to look this up. Where are the emergency numbers? Here it is 684-3752. Dial it slow so you get through," said Kimberly.

All right, here goes, 6-8-4-3-7-5-2; it is going through?," said Eric excitedly.

"Hello, this is the Fifth Precinct, can we help you?," said the officer.

"Yes, my name is Eric Shaw and I'm calling from the Mercy General Hospital. We, I mean my wife and I, have just lost a baby not quite two days ago," said Eric.

"I'm sorry to hear that, but what does that have to do with this emergency number call?," said the officer.

"We have found out that they want to use our baby for body parts and she is to be taken away around one-thirty in the morning. She and other babies like her are in the basement of this hospital. They are suppose to go to Noitcnas Laboratory for autopsies. This is a farce. They are taking them to another place. Please, you've got to help us!," begged Eric.

"Are you sure about this? Have you been reading some kind of science fiction novel? Is this some kind of Joke?," asked the officer.

"I know that this sounds bizarre, but this is the truth! Look, just have this number traced, we are calling from the hospital. We are frantic because there are only a few hours left to save her! I'll keep talking to you as you trace the call!," pleaded Eric.

"That won't be necessary. For some unknown reason deep in my gut, I believe that you are telling the truth. I will call this in and a patrol car will be over as soon as possible," said the officer.

"Thank you officer! And our baby thanks you!," said Eric.

As soon as the officer hung up Eric was going to walk around the bed to put the phone back on the stand, when he heard another click on the telephone line. Fear went through his heart. Someone had to have been on the line and heard the whole conversation. But all he could do was put the phone back on the hook.

Chapter XI

Covering A Foul Deed

"Kimberly, someone was on the line and listened in! Go out into the corridor and make up an excuse to see who is at the front desk. I'll stand behind the door so as not to be seen," said Eric.

Kimberly got up and put her robe and slippers on quickly and went out into the corridor and closed the door. She walked slowly down the corridor towards the front desk, so as not to look suspicious.

"Why, hello Kimberly! What are you doing out so late tonight? You don't want to overdo yourself and get your strength down or cause those stiches to tear," said Doctor Corona.

"I just wanted to go into the nursery to see Eric Junior before I retire. That way, if I know he is fine then I'll go on to bed," said Kimberly.

Kimberly felt Doctor Corona' eyes watch her every move. She went into the nursery and there was little Eric sucking his fingers. Such a sweetheart. Then she went back and returned to her room.

She closed the door; "Eric it was Doctor Corona and I know he knows everything. What are we to do? Hope the Patrol car gets here soon," said Kimberly anxiously.

Click went the door. Kimberly tried to open it, but it was locked. Eric tried to open it, but it was no use. Those hospital doors are just too thick. Eric tried the phone, it was dead. He knew that if they did not get out of there soon, they might never see their Tara again.

"Eric let's try the heating vents in the ceiling. You might be able to get through them. Pull the chair over by them and if that isn't high enough for you to reach, use the phone stand also. Hurry Eric, I am really scared!," said Kimberly frantically.

"That might just do it Kimberly! Hold the stand still for me. Ah, yes, it will work! I want you to listen at the door for the nurse. Nurse! We haven't tried the call button by the bed! See if it works! I'll climb down and wait about five minutes. If no one comes, we will know that he has done something to that also," said Eric.

Eric and Kimberly waited for nurse response, but not patiently. Each paced around watching their watches. When they had given up hope, Eric climbed back up on the chair and stand, with Kimberly holding the stand. They heard footsteps; they heard a click at the door!

In walked a nurse. "What is going on in here? What are you doing up there anyway? Why was your door locked? I noticed that when I came on my rounds to check in, that your phone and room button had been disconnected. What is this all about?," asked the nurse.

Eric no sooner tried to explain, but when in walked the police. They saw the chair and stand and also wanted to know just what was going on. The nurse told them what she had found at the front desk and about the locked door. The police asked Eric what he wanted to do about this situation. Eric told them to all head to the basement, if they were not to late.

The elevator door opened up and they all went down to the basement. Into the main corridor to four and to six. They went down five rooms and the Shaw name had been removed. The two other babies were gone too. They sure wrapped everything up nice and easy and neat, as they say.

Eric ran to the basement loading door and the police followed him. Faintly in a distant outside, Eric spotted a green van with a silver line across the back door.

"Sorry Mr. Shaw, but there is no evidence of any babies down here. You can still file a complaint to the hospital and get another investigation going inquiring about the episode in your wife's room. We will ask some questions upstairs, but I can tell you that now it is really out of our hands," said the officer.

"Wait! Get hold of Nurse Low first before you go. She will tell you that there was a baby of ours in the basement to be ready to be sent to the laboratory. We were to make up our minds first. They did not have our consent. Please do this, not for me, but for my wife! This has been a nightmare!," said Eric angerly.

Kimberly was on the brink of crying hysterically, but she fought against it like a champ. The police consented to go on ahead to call Nurse Low as soon as they got upstairs. Everyone proceeded to leave corridor six, back into corridor four, and into the elevator. It seemed an eternity getting back up to their floor, this time.

The officer called Nurse Low from the front desk. She lived about thirty minutes away from the hospital. The officer said that they would wait. The nurse on duty allowed them to wait there at the front desk. She said that she would bring up some coffee from the cafeteria for all of them.

While they were waiting, who should appear, but Doctor Corona. He acted as though nothing had happened. Eric and Kimberly looked at him and the police with utter disbelief.

"Hello, I'm Doctor Corona, officers. Is there something that I can help you with? Kimberly and Eric, you look very distraught. Is there something wrong? Is there something wrong that I should know about Eric Junior?," asked Doctor Corona.

Eric Junior! Kimberly and Eric yelled. And they ran straight into the nursery.

"Thank goodness he is all right! I thought for sure there for a minute that Doctor Corona had taken him from us too!," yelled Eric.

They went out of the nursery then and back to the front desk. The officers were still talking to Doctor Corona. Seems that the good doctor was trying to convince them that Kimberly and Eric had been under a lot of stress the last couple of days. And the good doctor hoped that the officers understood.

Eric intervened in the conversation. He asked the police what they thought about the episode in room three. They agreed that something was not ruled out yet as a criminal misdeed. Then Eric asked the police if they still were going to wait for Nurse Low. They said that they would. So everyone sat down again including Doctor Corona.

There was kind of a dead silence for the rest of the half hour. The only thing that broke the silence was when the nurse brought up the coffee for Doctor Corona.

Finally Nurse Low arrived. The police took her into another room to ask her questions. This left Kimberly and Eric and Doctor Corona, because the nurse on duty left for her rounds.

"You will never get away with this foul deed! We will find proof to put you and Doctor Mecht away. We will never give up!," said Eric threatening.

"The only thing I can't figure out is how the parents get the babies back. Nurse Low has told us that. Unless you take out the parts and then send the babies back," said Kimberly.

The police came back in with Nurse Low. Nurse Low told Doctor Corona to get Doctor Mecht so they could get this settled and put an end to all this. Doctor Corona was gone only about fifteen minutes when he came back with Doctor Mecht. Nurse Low told everyone that they were going to go down to the basement. They would be shown where Tara was being kept safe until they would have Kimberly's and Eric's consent.

"We were down in the basement earlier and Tara was gone! They had both seen her body earlier plus two other babies. They were gone also. It is impossible that they took them away in a van out of the basement loading zone unnoticed!," said Eric.

They all walked down to the elevator and got inside. Not much conversation inside, just glares. Once that they were in the basement they went down the same corridor into corridor four, to corridor six. They walked down to only number two room and there was the name Shaw on the door.

"This cannot be! Someone is playing a bad heartless joke on us. This is very cruel and sick!," cried out Kimberly.

They all went inside. There were three babies. All had tags on their feet. They were not in tubs, nor did they have breathing apparatus in their noses. Kimberly and Eric saw the name Tara on one of the tags. Kimberly and Eric walked on over to that baby. Eric picked up her forefinger, there was a number there. This baby looked like Tara, but they knew better.

The police said it was all a misunderstanding and hoped that this did not cause too much of an inconvenience. They thought that the doctors might give Kimberly and Eric some help so that their imaginations would not get out of hand.

Doctor Corona stayed behind along with Doctor Mecht. They said that they might as well stay and do a check on the babies since they were down there already. They told the police that Nurse Low would see that Kimberly got back to her room and that Eric could go home.

So they all left and went down the corridors into the elevator and back to the nursery floor. Nurse Low told Eric that he might as well go home and stop in to see Kimberly early tomorrow. As they still need to make a decision about the Noitcnas Laboratory. Whatever they decided would be fine. She also said that she would make sure that Kimberly was taken care of.

Eric told Nurse Low that first he would like to say something to Kimberly privately. She consented to that. Kimberly and Eric went into room three and closed the door.

"Kimberly, I don't want you to go off this floor. Keep an eye on Eric Junior for me. I will handle the situation and I will see you early tomorrow morning," said Eric.

"I will stay on this floor and we will be fine, and take care Eric," said Kimberly.

Chapter XII

A Calm Day?

When Eric left the hospital he went home. It was about an hour's drive from the hospital. When he got to his house he remembered that he had not fed the dog. So once inside, he got the can of dog food out of the cupboard and went out back to feed Roggow, the beautiful black lab. Eric patted the dog and gave him a big hug because he felt guilty for not giving him attention these last few days. That wasn't the only reason though, he needed some reassurance himself.

Back inside Eric got some clean clothes out so he could take a shower. He thought maybe he would feel better once he was cleaned up. He also needed to relax and get his mind clear for some serious thought on the whole problem.

Kimberly couldn't sleep. She watched the time and every hour she would walk out in the hall into the nursery and check Eric Junior. This went on until about four in the morning before Kimberly finally fell asleep.

Back home Eric had fallen asleep on the couch. He woke up with a jolt during another bad dream about Tara. He looked at the clock and it was after four-thirty a.m. He decided not to go back to the hospital until around eight. He would need to get more proof about all this and get Kimberly and Eric Junior home before taking any more action. He did decide one thing though, that would help, and he would let Kimberly know about it later in the morning. Right now he was going back to sleep until about seven. He went into the bedroom and brought out the alarm and set it.

During this time Doctor Corona and Doctor Mecht were getting upset with the trouble that Kimberly and Eric were giving them. They decided that they would dismiss Kimberly and the baby. This would get her and Eric out of the hospital and from all their interfering. Then they would dispose of the three babies as soon as possible. This would need to be done after Nurse Low was off duty.

Kimberly woke up when breakfast was being brought in. She didn't care about breakfast right then. She got up out of bed and shoved the tray away dropping her coffee cup. She scurried as fast as she could into the nursery.

"Where is he? Nurse! Nurse! Where is my baby? What have they done with him? Tell me!," yelled Kimberly hysterically.

"What is all this yelling about? Kimberly, I just had gone into the other room opposite the nursery to give little Eric Junior a bath. He spit up all over his clothes this morning. See, he is just fine! Only thing is wrong with him, is that he is wide awake and very hungry," said Nurse Low.

"I was just so upset. I thought for sure Eric Junior was gone! I am terribly sorry Nurse Low! Can I go ahead and take him into my room for his feeding?," asked Kimberly.

"Yes, I'll bring in the formula in a couple of minutes. Tell the other nurse that I said it will be all right with me," said Nurse Low.

Kimberly went into her room and sat down in the rocking chair. She held Eric Junior tightly, then she kissed him profusely. She was so glad that he was safe. In walked Nurse Low with the bottle. She handed it to Kimberly. Kimberly put it into Eric's mouth and he began sucking on it furiously. It did not take him long to be fed and burped. The young nurse came in to get the tray. She asked Kimberly if anything was wrong.

"Not now, anyway," said Kimberly.

"Do you want me to get you more coffee and leave the tray longer?," asked the young nurse.

"Would you! That would be so nice," said Kimberly.

"When I bring the coffee, I will put the baby back into the nursery. He looks as if he is sound asleep," said the young nurse.

"Yes he is asleep, after a full tummy," said Kimberly.

Just then in walked Doctor Corona. He was all smiles today. Evil knows all tricks of the trade.....thought Kimberly.

"Hello Kimberly, how are you today? I have good news for you! You and Eric Junior can go home today right after lunch. Remember to sign out in the office. I will be back later this morning and see you again before you leave," said Doctor Corona.

Kimberly never said a thing. She sat there and listened and turned her head. She did not have to look at him. As he left, in walked Eric. He bent over and kissed Kimberly and Eric Junior.

Chapter XIII

Consent

"Is that all he does is sleep? I would hold him but I do not want to wake him up," said Eric.

"Doctor Corona was in, as you saw. He said that we can go home after lunch. We need to sign out at the front desk before we leave," said Kimberly.

"Good! That resolves one of my problems," said Eric.

Then in walked the young nurse with Kimberly's coffee. She sat it down on the tray, went over to Kimberly and took Eric Junior back to the nursery.

"Haven't you eaten yet? Why don't you sit down and eat and I will tell you about what I have decided to do," said Eric.

"Oh, all right, I was intending to eat anyway, silly. Now please close the door before you start telling me," said Kimberly.

Eric got up and checked the corridor before he closed the door. Then he sat down on the bed beside Kimberly and started talking.

"We are going to consent to having Tara sent to the Noitcnas Laboratory. Even though we know that she is already there. The baby that is going is not her. Trust me, we will find Tara and help out other people's children also. Now we will talk more about this at home," said Eric.

"This is it! There is no more after all we have gone through here," said Kimberly angrily.

"The main thing right now is to get you both home safely. The next important thing to do is give our decision to Doctor Corona. This is so he will think that we are giving up. Now Kimberly, you should know that I would never give up," said Eric.

"I really did know that deep down inside of my heart. Please forgive me Eric, for ever doubting you!," said Kimberly.

After Kimberly finished breakfast and talking with Eric, she started to pack. She had to leave one suitcase open, because she couldn't change into street clothes until after Doctor Corona had examined her. She wished that he would hurry so she wouldn't have need for him again. She was going to change doctors and maybe hospitals too. She was glad that Eric was there early, today.

Eric had settled down and had turned on the television and the news report came on. The headlines read, Human Fetal-Cell Transplants Planned. It went on and talked about the moral and the ethical issues involved. Scientists agreed that conventional medicine determines human death on the basis of total brain failure. How, then, can we remove living tissues from a dead brain? It went on and they talked about using the aborted fetus. They were afraid that it may become a marketable product. Eric was going to listen to more, when, Doctor Corona walked in. Eric got up and shut off the television.

"Eric would you step out in the hall while I examine Kimberly? Please close the door behind you. Well, Kimberly, let's have a look. Stiches are about dissolved and everything else looks fine. I am going over to the nursery and give Eric Junior a check too before you go. Eric, you can come in now," said Doctor Corona.

"Eric, please go on over to the nursery while Doctor Corona is checking Eric Junior. I would feel a lot better if you would," said Kimberly.

"Okay, see you in a little bit," said Eric.

"He is doing just fine and is a strong healthy boy. By the way, what did you decide about Tara?," asked Doctor Corona.

"Kimberly and I have decided it would be best if we did consent to her going to Noitcnas Laboratory. How long will it take to get her back, so we can make funeral arrangements?," asked Eric.

"I would say, you had better give them about three weeks or more. Then when they are done with the test results of the autopsy, I will notify you myself," said Doctor Corona.

"We will be waiting," said Eric.

Eric waited until Doctor Corona had left the nursery before he went back into Kimberly's room. He wanted to make sure that Doctor Corona was not around while he talked to Kimberly.

Kimberly had changed into her street clothes. They fit a little snugly. She had gained more than what she had thought. She knew for sure now that she wasn't going to eat all her lunch today. She thought to herself that she had better cut down on the eating a bit.

"I had a little chat with the good doctor while I was in the nursery. I told him that we decided to let Tara go to the Noitcnas Laboratory. He said that it would be three weeks or more before we get the results. He didn't look too surprised at all about our decision," said Eric.

"Why should he be? He knows that we have no proof to stop him," said Kimberly.

Kimberly was cut short because the young nurse brought in Eric Junior for his next feeding. He was sucking his fingers again. The young nurse handed him to Kimberly who had just sat down in the rocking chair. Kimberly eagerly took the baby in her arms tenderly. The young nurse gave her the bottle. Kimberly carefully put the bottle into Eric Junior's mouth. Now as he was contented and

55

settled down, the young nurse told them that they did not need him to be taken back to the nursery. They were to ring for her and she would bring in the wheelchair for Kimberly to be dismissed when they were finished. Then they could stop at the front desk and sign out. They didn't need to stay for lunch. Eric thanked her.

"I will be glad when we are out of here," he said.

"I will agree with that wholeheartedly," said Kimberly.

"It won't take him long to finish his bottle. So far he is still dry; I can always change him on the way home. Would you check the drawers and the closets and also the bathroom, to see if I have left anything, Eric?," asked Kimberly.

"All right, I'll do that now, let's see, yes the drawers are empty and the closet is oh, oh, your slippers. Now to the bathroom, nothing here. And your luggage, I will set it by the door," said Eric.

"He has finished now; I will burp him. Goodness! What a burp for someone so small. Eric, go on ahead and ring for the nurse," said Kimberly.

Eric got up again and rang for the young nurse. He helped Kimberly wrap up Eric Junior in a bigger blanket. By that time the young nurse was there.

"Everyone ready to go home? Eric why don't you take the baby and Kimberly can get into the wheelchair. Then hand back the baby while I wheel her out to the front desk ahead of you. Then you can bring the suitcases," said the young nurse.

"See You in a little bit," said Eric.

The nurse pushed Kimberly and Eric Junior slowly up to the front desk. Then she went around the desk to get the papers that needed to be signed for their release. It took her awhile to find them. By that time Eric had caught up with them. Kimberly and Eric signed the papers. Eric then needed to go down and get the car out of the parking lot and pull it up to the hospital entrance. Also to take the luggage down to the car. The nurse said that she would wait with Kimberly until he got back.

"Just thought that you should know that today is when they will be taking Tara to the Noitcnas Laoratory. I think that two more babies are going as well. I want you to know that I am sorry about what happened. You at least have a baby to take home. Most do not! It is so heartbreaking to see those parents leaving the hospital, alone," said the young nurse.

Eric came back up and was all smiles. He wanted to push Kimberly in the wheelchair, but the nurse said no, hospital rules. So he followed alongside until they went down eight floors and it brought them to the main entrance. A sigh of relief went out of Kimberly as they went out the door. This time the nurse took the baby while Kimberly got inside of the car. She handed Eric Junior back to Kimberly. Eric closed the door and walked around to the other side of the car to get in. They waved to the nurse and drove off.

Chapter XIV

Homeward Bound

It was a nice hourly drive home. Kimberly enjoyed the freeway sight. Anything was better than the hospital. One would think that a ride on the freeway would not be a tension reliever. It was for Kimberly and Eric.

"Eric, while you were getting the car, the nurse told me that today, still, they were going to send Tara and the other babies to the Noitcnas Laboratory. That means that we get no rest today, right?," asked Kimberly.

"We will talk about that as soon as we get home which is in a few minutes. Well, does it look the same? I bet that Roggow has really missed you!," said Eric.

"Roggow! I completely forgot all about him. Have you fed him and let him in the house?," asked Kimberly.

"Fed him yes, let him in the house, no," said Eric.

"That is all right! I think I will let him in to get used to the baby," said Kimberly.

They drove into the driveway and stopped in the front of the door entrance. Eric got out to unlock the house. Then he came back and opened the door for Kimberly, walking up to the house door and opening that for Kimberly. While he opened the trunk for the suitcases, he noticed a piece of paper fall back inside the trunk after he had set them on the ground. He reached for the piece of paper to get a look at it. On the paper was written Sanction B&F 9826, the rest of the paper was ripped away. The bottom of the paper had a label refill and a place where the doctor was to sign. This was a prescription paper, he thought. Placing the paper, folded, into his pocket, he closed the trunk and took the suitcases into the house.

He got Kimberly and the baby settled, told Kimberly that he had to go to watch the hospital basement entrance. He had to find out where they were taking all these babies. This could take quite awhile. But first, go to the store to get food and formula and diapers. Kimberly said that it was fine, so Eric left.

Kimberly went into the laundry room to put in a load of clothes into the washer. She also went into the kitchen and put the dishes into the dishwasher. She had thought of vacuuming, but she didn't want to overdo it for today, so she decided to go into the bedroom and change her sheets. That didn't take long, so she put another load of laundry into the washer and headed for the nursery. It looked like everything was fine and Eric Junior was still asleep. So she decided to go into the living room to watch the television.

Eric was gone about an hour an a half. When he came home he noticed a car follwing him. He pulled into his driveway got out of his car. He carried the groceries and other things into the house, looked out his kitchen window and noticed the same car......pulling away from his house, very slowly and leaving.

Eric then put away a tv-dinner into the freezer for Kimberly for her supper tonight, then put the rest of the groceries away for her and the formula and the diapers.

Eric went outside and got Roggow and put him inside the house. He told Kimberly to leave the dog inside while he was gone. He also told Kimberly to lock the doors. He would call her as soon as he found something out.

She said that she would be fine. She thought that she might call Wanda, her best friend, to come over for awhile. Wanda didn't live too far from their place.

"Just please, please, be careful and call the police if the need be. Maybe I should go with you?," asked Kimberly.

"No, you stay right here so I won't worry about both of you. Love you Kimberly!," said Eric.

Chapter XV

Seeking Proof

Eric went out and got into his car. He did not see the car that had followed him as he headed toward the hospital. Nor did he see that car during the hour drive to the hospital. He pulled around in the back of the hospital by the basement entrance, making sure that no one had seen him pull up back by the garbage dumpster. His car could not be seen; it was small enough to be hidden. A vehicle coming down the alley would notice him in the daytime but not later towards the evening. He had to get back inside to make sure that the babies were still inside. He hoped that they were and that he didn't miss the van.

He got out of his car and walked up carefully to the door entrance, which was right by the driveway entrance. Thank goodness there was no one around either entrance at that time. Once inside he looked for the corridor signs. He had to go north this time to corridor six. He walked cautiously and then there was a sign saying D.O.A.'s, aborted, accidental and unknown. He went down that corridor for the unknowns, walked into room two and there were the three babies, yet. Turning around he checked the corridor to see if anyone was coming. He knew that he needed to put some kind of identification on the baby that was tagged Tara. This way he could prove that this was not Tara to the police. He went into the closet and was looking when he found a pair of scissors and a label machine. He got out the labeler and printed out, unknown. He then cut this out and placed this inside her mouth as he had done to the real Tara. He then put the scissors and the labeler back inside the closet and closed the door.

Then he got out a piece of paper from his wallet and wrote down these numbers......331, 332, 333, before putting the piece of paper inside his wallet. No sooner had he done that, when he heard voices. He cautiously checked out in the corridor. He saw no one, but the voices were getting louder, so they were getting closer. He sneaked into the room across the corridor, the one that had no light on. He then crawled up to the door opening, so he could see what was going on. He saw this......

"Doctor Mecht, do you want me to put the babies in each of the cold storage crates or all in one large one?," asked the orderly.

"Put each into a separate crate and watch the temperature.

I want you to stay here with me because the van should be here in about thirty minutes. I need your help in cleaning up some instruments after I use them on the babies. I need to take some blood samples and et cetera, you know, the normal routine again," said Doctor Mecht.

"I'll go down to room ten and be back with the crates and I'll turn on the temperature gages on each one. Then I'll help you load up each baby and next I'll clean the instruments and change the small sheets on the gurneys," said the orderly.

"That will be fine, I should have everything done by the time that you get back," said Doctor Mecht.

Eric watched the orderly leave down the corridor. He could see Doctor Mecht clearly. He took out three needles and began to draw blood from each of the babies. He then put the blood from each of the babies into a small tube. And labeled these with each number of the babies. He checked the temperature of each baby and did other things which Eric really did not understand what they were for.

Soon the orderly came in and he pulled three crates. Doctor Mecht checked the temperature and then they lifted each of the babies in a crate and put the blood sample in beside each of them. The orderly closed the crates and started to clean up.

Eric heard a van pull up to the entrance. It must be the same van, he thought to himself. Two men came walking up the corridor with uniforms on. On the back of their shirts was printed Noitcnas Laboratory. He carefully got out a piece of paper from his wallet. A pen from his shirt pocket and jotted that name down. The two men then pulled the crates down the corridor and into the loading zone. Eric could not see them actually loading the babies into the van. He could not risk being seen.

Doctor Mecht told the orderly he could leave and go back upstairs. He had told the two men to wait for him before they left. He needed them to sign a paper.

Eric tried to sneak out of the room, but it was impossible. He strained his hearing as far as possible to determine what was being said.

"You know what to do with these three babies. Just standard procedure boys. I need you to sign this so I can put it into the file so it will be cleared," said Doctor Mecht.

"We understand and when can we expect to come back again?," said one of the men.

"I'll get hold of B&F and they will let you know," said Doctor Mecht.

Doctor Mecht headed for the elevator to go upstairs. The men closed the doors on the van. Then they got inside to leave.

Eric knew that he had better hurry if he was going to find out where they took Tara. He looked to see if Doctor Mecht was in the elevator, and he was. So he left the room cautiously, but a lot faster than when he had come in. The van had just pulled away. He now was running toward the door. His heart was pounding. He got outside into his car, where he had left the keys in the ignition thank goodness. He started the car and peeled out.

Chapter XVI

The Chase

Eric noticed in the rear view mirror that they went down the alley. So he sped down the alleyway, too. He caught a glimpse of the van far ahead. He had to stop at the intersection. If he had been the first one at the stop light he would have gone ahead right on through the red light. He was perspiring now as he peeled out and he could barely see the van now. He passed cars, right and left, to get ahead of the traffic. He saw the van turn left. He needed to get to the corner, but a truck pulled in front of him yelled a lot of insinuations at him. He knew that he had probably lost the van.

The man in the truck stepped out and came up to the car door. The man was very large and muscular. The man stooped down to his car window. Eric was terrified; this man was huge. Eric rolled down his window and told the man he thought that he was going to have a coronary and was hurrying to the hospital. The man believed him and moved his truck out of his way. Actually that was not a total lie to tell the man, as he really felt as if he could have had one! Off Eric sped to the next corner and turned left.

No van! Not anywhere! Eric went around in circles for awhile hoping that they had stopped somewhere nearby. No luck! He was about to give up hope, when he saw the van about five blocks down. He was attempting to speed off again when he heard a siren behind him and a light went on by him. Yes! It was the police! Eric pulled over to stop. Another car pulled up beside him. Eric recognized the car. It was the same one that had followed him home. He wondered what this was all about.

"Are You Eric Shaw?," asked the detective holding out his badge.

"Yes, I am," said Eric.

"Would you please step over here and get into that car?," pointed the policeman.

"What is this all about?," asked Eric.

"We will fill you in on the details as we go to find the van," said the detective.

"The green van with the silver stripe on the back doors?," asked Eric.

"That is the one!," said the detective.

The detective told Eric that they had been after that van for a long time. They had been following Eric to see if he had found out any more than they had on the van. Plus that they had wanted to make sure that he was in no kind of trouble, so they had followed.

Eric had told him what had happened when he had called the police the first time at the hospital. He also told them that was when he had first caught a glimpse of the van. He then told them that he had sneaked back into the hospital, giving them all the information on that.

They knew most of what he said was true. They said the reason they didn't do more to the doctors was that they needed more proof. But the detective did want Eric to know that they had taken fingerprints secretly from the front desk phone and the doorknob to his wife's room at the hospital. The fingerprints turned out to be Doctor Corona's. Anyway, he was the only one to have access to unhook the phone that night. The young nurse didn't know how to unhook them because she had to ask Doctor Corona to put them back in working order.

"We need to fine out where the van takes the babies and the name of the laboratory. We can't seem to find an address for the name, Noitcnas," said the detective.

"You say it was written on their uniforms, so it must be a legitimate place somewhere around here," said the detective.

As luck would have it, they spotted the van. It seemed unusual that there would be any laboratory in this direction. This was the direction for the lower east side. Only vacant factory buildings, and of course the dump site.

They got a closer look at the van before it turned again. This time the detective knew for sure that they were heading towards the dump site.

"We are going to go around the back way into the dump site and hide the car. We can do it hopefully without them seeing us," said the detective.

The driver turned their car around and went in the other direction to the dump site. They all watched out for the van, so as not to be seen. And pulled into and old shed on the dump site, cautiously, they all got out.

The two detectives decided to split up. They asked Eric if he wanted to go with one of them. He agreed to go with Detective Borges. The other detective's name was Reiber.

Reiber went ahead to the east and Borges and Eric went west. They heard a motor running, but it was only the salvage worker getting ready to crush a car. They moved on and walked on through a lot of stinking garbage. They moved up and down through five great mounds of the stuff......when......Eric spotted the van.

"Over there behind the stacked tires, don't you see it?," said Eric.

"Yes I do, now I wonder if Reiber has caught a glimpse of the van also," said Detective Borges.

They moved a little closer without being seen. They saw to their horror, the two men taking the crates out of the van and lifting the babies out and wrapping them up with and old garbage bag. The two men placed each of the babies in a different spot under piles of garbage. No wonder the bodies of the other babies were never found, if this had been done before. The men put back the crates in the van and left.

"Did you see any of the men take out and destroy the blood samples that were taken? They were by each of the babies in a small glass tube," said Eric.

"I did not see them destroy anything like that," said Detective Borges.

Detective Reiber took a little while walking through the garbage before he got to Eric and Detective Borges.

"Did you see the two men take out any blood samples in tubes being destroyed?," asked Detective Borges.

"No sir, I did not, unless they did that before we noticed them taking out the crates," said Detective Reiber.

"We will have to go back to the car and call all this in and mention the blood samples and see if they find them. That may mean a clue of some kind," said Detective Borges.

They headed back to the car, having to walk again over the enormous mounds of garbage. By now their shoes really did stink and were caked with dirt and gunk. When they got to the car Detective Borges called in the report. Eric and Detective Reiber sat down inside the car and waited until Detective Borges got finished on the radio.

Eric wondered to himself why they didn't put a report on the van. Just as soon as that thought passed his mind Detective Borges called in a report, an all-out bulletin lookout on the van. Then Detective Borges talked to Eric.

"I really don't know where to look for the van. Guess we can go on out with the rest of the men and drive around this area. My guess is that they are gone by now and have hidden the van," said Detective Borges.

Chapter XVII

The Search

Eric tried to reason as to why hadn't they been able to find an address on this Noitcnas. He wanted to know just how long they had been trying.

"We have been trying for the past year. We cannot find this Noitcnas because the listing says that they have either moved or their old address is an old empty Warehouse that has not been used for years. No babies have really disappeared because the parents do get their babies back after the autopsy is done. So when you told the police about their trying to take your baby without your consent, you can now understand our interest in this," said Detective Borges.

"So we have these questions to be answered then. To find the real location of Noitcnas, to find out what they do to the babies, and to find out why those babies were killed and the question about their blood," said Detective Reiber.

This time Detective Reiber drove the car. They drove into the driveways of most of the warehouses and the old factories. They all got out to have a look inside of each one to see if the van was inside. They did this for about an hour before Detective Borges told them to stop.

"I say it is time to quit looking around here. They have gone. Pull over and let's put all three heads together and see if we can come up with something," said Detective Borges.

They pulled the car over at an empty warehouse near the edge of town. It was kind of a break because they could get out and stretch and look out and see the bridge; the water was simply beautiful!

"Is there anything at all that you might have missed or left out that you haven't told us Eric?," asked Detective Borges.

Eric ran over all the circumstances through his brain again. He went through and relived every minute of it in his mind. Reiber and Borges stepped out of the car to give him time to do his thinking.

Eric remembered that he had forgotten to tell them two important facts. He got out of the car and walked on down toward the bridge toward the detectives.

"I remember that after I took Kimberly home and went back outside to get the luggage, when I lifted them up, a piece of paper fell back into the trunk. It must have gotten caught on the suitcase clasp near the bottom. I still have it in my back pocket. I hope! Yes! See it says Sanction B&F 9826 on it. As you can see it is a prescription paper. Maybe we can find out whose handwriting it is?," said Eric.

"That will take sometime, because someone will have to go back to the hospital and get the doctors handwriting, so we can compare it to this note. Let me look at this again. I wonder if this 9826 is part of the address or a phone number?," asked Detective Reiber.

"I am going to call this in on the radio to see if they can help us find an address or some kind of information on this. I will be back," said Detective Borges.

"Keep going over things in your mind Eric, you may have some more information that we need," said Detective Reiber.

Eric decided to walk along the bridge now and think. He knew that it was getting late and he would need to call Kimberly. If only he could remember something else of importance. He got out his wallet to see if he had put anything in there of importance. He found the numbers of the babies he had written down. He also remembered B&F being mentioned by Doctor Mecht. Then he turned back and headed to the car and so did Detective Reiber. Detective Borges was on his way to get them when he saw them coming so he returned to the car and got in.

Eric and Detective Reiber reached the car and got inside. Detective Borges was going to start the car and leave, when Eric said to them that he wanted to talk before they left.

"Here are the numbers of the babies that were dumped. I had written them down when I sneaked into the basement. Could they have the real babies with these same numbers at the laboratory? I overheard Doctor Mecht talking to the man in the van that B&F will get back to him as to when they can come again. So this piece of paper with Sanction B&F has got to be the place where my Tara is. You see the baby that was dumped was not my Tara, I have proof of that," said Eric.

"What proof is that?," asked Detective Reiber.

"When I find Tara I will show you," said Eric.

Eric then took out a piece of paper from his wallet and a pen from his shirt pocket. He wrote down Noitcnas and then Sanction. He first counted the letters. Each word did have eight letters in it. The detective watched with curiousity. Then Eric printed Sanction and right below it he printed Noitcnas. Both words had the same letters.

"See this Noitcnas is Sanction spelled backwards. But I wonder just what B&F stand for?," asked Eric.

"That is terrific Eric! That really is great proof," exclaimed Detective Borges.

So Detective Borges called in the bulletin for the address for Sanction B&F. Soon over the radio, the dispatcher gave Detective Borges the address. It is 9826 Boulevard 23 and North Central.

"Before we go to find the address, can you have someone call my wife and let her know that I am fine and that I am with both of you detectives? My number is 334-7762," said Eric.

This time Detective Reiber called that in for Eric. After that, they left for 23 Boulevard and North Central. That was about four miles from where they were.

"Is anyone getting hungry? I know I am, so how about pulling over to a gas station and letting me get us some candy bars," said Detective Reiber.

"That sounds good. I want a Babruth. What kind do you want Eric?," asked Detective Borges.

"I will take a zero bar, thank you," said Eric.

So Detective Borges pulled the car over to a Texaco station. Detective Reiber went inside to get the candy bars. Soon he came out and away they continued to their destination.

The traffic was getting heavy because most people were getting off from work. Their ride seemed forever before getting off the freeway. Soon Eric noticed a sign for North Central. They had to go down to 23rd street now. Eric counted the streets under his breath. They finally got to 23rd.

They turned off the freeway into 23rd and drove slowly to the addresses reading as they went in order.

They figured out that to get to the nine hundred block, that they needed to turn east from the eight hundred block. Okay, so now they have gotten on the right street. 9820...... 9823...... there it was......9826.

Chapter XVIII

Finally Located

It was a smaller building than what they had expected. It was three stories tall and an older brick building, in between two older warehouses. All looked as if they were used only for storage. In the front of the building there was the name on a large metal plaque; it read SANCTION B&F.

There seemed to be no one around the front, anyway. There were no cars. It was starting to get late and there seemed to be only a small entrance light on. There could be a guard inside and probably there are more lights on inside. Maybe they should go around the back or find some kind of an opening to get in. These were the three mens thoughts.

"Let's go on around to the back and find a place to park the car. Somewhere it cannot be seen. Then we can go on foot and check out this building and see if there is some way we can enter it without being noticed," said Detective Borges.

"That sounds good to me. How about you, Eric?," asked Detective Reiber.

"I think that we really need to keep on our guard. It looks too easy. Could it be a trap? Or is it going to be a hard puzzle when we get inside? And are we talking major violence here?," asked Eric.

"We really just don't know. We have to get inside to see. This may be our only chance. If we flub up on this one, they may move their whole operation somewhere else," said Detective Borges.

So they went around back and parked the car in the alley in between two buildings where there were no street lights. They then walked over to the Sanction B&F Building's back entrance. There were two cars there. Inside they could see a light in the bottom story. Walking around to the right side of the building, they found a small opening by the garbage bin. Above that was a window with an old screen, one that hadn't been attended to for some time.

The men climbed up on the garbage bin and took off the screen with Eric's pocket knife. They then looked to see how this older window was latched. They then decided to break the window. Detective Borges took off his jacket and wrapped it around his hand gently but firmly, pushed it against the glass until it broke. He unlatched the window and pushed it open. Shaking the glass from his jacket he put it back on. He was the first to go inside. It was dark, but he managed not to fall or make noise. He put a chair over near the window for the other men to use to get inside.

Reiber went next. He snagged his tie on a nail and it made a loud rip noise. They waited to see if anyone had heard that.

Eric was last. He made it in with no trouble. He had a time with his eyes adjusting to the dark, once inside.

Now all inside this room, they decided that they had better split up again. This way they could cover more territory. Detective Borges looked down the hallway to see if anyone was around. No one as yet, thank goodness! Detective Borges decided that he would take the top floor, Detective Reiber the second floor, and Eric the first floor. They were to meet in this room. They were to get proof of some kind. Try to avoid violence if possible.

Eric waited for Detective Borges to leave first. Then he waited for Detective Reiber to leave next. Then he would go out behind them.

Eric walked out cautiously. He did not know what to expect. Down the hallway was a room with a light on. He hoped that no one was in that room. He slowly walked up next to the door, opened it, and looked inside. This room was full of computers and files only. He went up to a file and looked up the name Shaw, to see if he could find out anything. He opened the drawer and went through them. No luck in that file cabinet. He went on over to another one. He noticed that this file cabinet, on the front, said unknown. He knew that this had to be the right one.

Chapter XIX

More Foul Deeds

He found the s's and found the name Shaw, Tara. They were not actually supposed to have her name, only a number, he thought. Anyway, that is what Nurse Low had told them. He read on further and it said that she was on the third floor. It said that they needed to try to keep her alive to see if they could graft brain tissue from an older newborn as they have done from a fetus. This was to be used on a person who had Parkinson's disease. They also needed her brain tissue to try on an Alzheimer's patient. They also want to see if implants from her nerve cells will grow once used inside a stroke victim.

"This is monstrous!," thought Eric.

As he read on, he found out that she wasn't really brain dead totally. She was given an injection of Phenacetin. This drug induces excessive breakdowns of red blood cells. This is said to cause brain damage, but they didn't check for the full extent.

"That means that part of her brain is still functioning. I've got to get her out of here," thought Eric.

He cautiously went out of the room and down the hall. He didn't want to take the elevator. So he used the stairs. He thought that he would go see how Reiber was doing, so he walked up the stairs. When he got to the door opening he stopped. He hit the floor fast. He didn't want to be seen through the door window. He heard a commotion outside the door. That means that there are other people here besides we three.

He waited for awhile and made sure; putting his ear to the door window. The coast was clear, so far!

"I wonder what is up on this floor anyway? At least the hallways are lighted up so you can at least read the signs," thought Eric.

Eric had spotted the sign for the second floor. It read that this was the D.O.A's. Just great! Everyone should go on an adventure like this and see dead people. What am I doing here? Well, I'm in this now, no turning back! Looks like there are six rooms to check out here. Hope that Detective Reiber shows up before I really need to go into all of them. Hope that I don't run into anyone else around here either," thought Eric.

Eric noticed the temperature change when he went inside room one. The light was dim; once inside, Eric closed the door.

He turned around to see to his horror......bodies. There were three rows of bodies on hooks covered in see-through bags. On the other side of the room were just parts of bodies, in freezer vats. There were livers, hearts, kidneys and even legs and arms. He was getting sick to his stomach, plus he was cold. He opened the large door to go out when, he noticed something on the floor. It was a piece of material. Red, and was torn, he knew he had seen the color before.

"This was Detective Reiber's tie color. He had gotten it caught on the nail getting inside of the window. He must be in this room," thought Eric as terror gripped at his heart.

Eric now shivering from the cold and fear inside him. He turned back around to go through the dead bodies on the hooks. He started with the first row, going through them slowly. None of these bodies were Detective Reibers. He then took a deep breath, and went through the second row. No sign of him there. He was hoping that he might be wrong, when he started the third row. But, there, in the third row, a face showing that he had been in grotesque pain, was Detective Reiber. Eric turned him around to see if he might still be alive. Eric noticed that the hook went in too deep for a possibility, for that.

Eric was scared now. He needed to protect himself. He checked Reiber's body for his gun. He put his hand inside of his vest and sure enough, it was still there. He swallowed hard and looked to see if it held anymore bullets. Yes, there was. Eric was really cold by now. He knew that he had to get out of the room.

Eric walked over to the large door; opened it carefully, and looked out; it seemed to be clear. He walked out slowly. Now his hands and feet were stinging. He put the gun inside his pocket for now, putting the bullets in the other pocket. He walked on down past two more rooms. He had no intention of going into them. Sweat beaded on his brow; he was scared to think what might happen; that is, if he would meet up with the person or persons in the building. He was almost up to the exit for the stairway, when he heard voices. He saw the restroom and darted inside.

The voices were getting closer. He knew he must hide. There were three latrines and three stalls inside. He hid in the last stall. Purposely he didn't close the stall's door all the way, and moved into the corner of the door where it joined and as he then stood on the toilet seat, placing his feet on the side with the door covering them.

In walked the two men. Their voices were familiar. These were the same men who drove the van. They must be the guards for the laboratory, also.

One man walked over by the last stall. Eric's heart stopped. He reached inside of his pocket for they gun. Boy, that was close! All the man wanted to do was to wash his hands.

The two men talked, saying that they needed to go to check out the first floor, they hadn't found anyone on the third. Anyway, they needed to put in more data into the computers, and the men left.

"Detective Borges might still be alive, if he is still up on the third floor," thought Eric.

He waited until he heard the rest room door close. Eric got down and went to the door. He put his head out of the door carefully, to look to see if they were gone. Yes! They were gone!

Moving outside into the hall, Eric walked over to the stair exit and went up. He hurried quietly up the stairs to floor three. He noticed the sign in the hallway. It read, 'Unknowns.' There were six rooms up here also. He walked up to room one and went inside. There to his horror were tables of fetus's in vats being kept alive. Some were older than others. All these were human beings wanting a chance to live! To Survive!

Eric went into room two. This was where they had cells growing and living in tubes. He had no idea as to what else was in there, and he really didn't want to know.

From there into room three. Here were the older fetus's and they were tagged for using special parts. Some were alive and sucking their thumbs. There was a surgical table in the middle of the room. Beside the table was a waste vat and it had a bloody cloth in it. Seems they had already gotten their parts from some already.

Eric moved inside room four. This room was like watching an old Boris Karloff and Frankenstein movie. Only today it was no longer fiction but real.

Eric had just two more rooms to go into. He was heading for room four when......

"Eric," whispered Detective Borges, "come over here to room six."

Eric walked over to room six and went inside. There were only three babies in this room. They were in those tubs and had respirators yet. Eric looked closely at each baby. He knew that this one was his Tara!

"This is my baby! We have to get her out of here! They are going to use her for terrible experiments!," said Eric.

"We cannot take her out of here yet. There are two men here that I know of and they are armed. I hid in that closet while they searched all the rooms. I was just going to leave, when I saw you," said Detective Borges.

"Detective Reiber, is dead. I saw him on the second floor. They killed him and hung him on a hook and froze him. These men are killers!," said Eric.

Sadness showed on Detective Borges's face. "He was a good man, that Reiber. He has a family, did you know that?," said Detective Borges.

"No, I did not know that. I'm sorry, from what I have seen of him, he seemed to be a nice guy," said Eric.

Chapter XX

Revenge

"We are going to have to go downstairs to the first floor and overpower these animals. Then we can call for backup and help," said Detective Borges.

"I guess that you are right. We had better take the stairs again. I overheard the men talking and they were going to check the first floor out. Then they said that they had some work to do with the computers down there," said Eric.

So both men headed for the stairs. It didn't take them long to get down the three flights of stairs. When they got to the last floor, they walked slowly up to the exit door. Detective Borges carefully looked out the door window to see if the hallway was clear. He motioned to Eric to follow him out into the hall.

"Room four is the room with the computers. It is on the other side of the hallway," said Eric.

"Then it is to room four. I will go in first and you come in after me. When we get to the doorway, hit the floor. We will try a sneak attack. Good luck!," said Detective Borges.

Detective Borges went to the doorway and down to the floor. In he went; Eric went to the doorway. He went down to the floor when......he heard a shot! He went inside and saw Detective Borges, upon the floor, holding his shoulder, farther inside the room.

The men turned around and saw him. Eric reached in his pocket......pulled out his gun......fired. He shot one of the men in the stomach. The other man was going to shoot, but Detective Borges shot him in the chest. The man he had shot, reached over to some kind of buzzer, before he passed out.

"Shut that damn thing off! It is some kind of a warning to the rest of these animals," said Detective Borges.

Eric raced over to the buzzer, shut it off, but no sooner did he do that when......the man he had shot...... shot at him again. Luckily he missed, and Detective Borges got him, right between the eyes!

"I think that we are even now; by the way, where did you get the gun?," asked Detective Borges.

"From Detective Reiber's body. I was sure that I would be needing some protection," said Eric.

"I am glad that you did take the gun. Or else I might not be here talking to you. Help me tie a hanky, to stop this bleeding," said Detective Borges.

"Is that too tight?," asked Eric.

"No that is just fine. Now help me over to the desk so I can use the phone," said Detective Borges.

Eric took him by the other shoulder and sat him down by the phone. Eric returned to look closer at the buzzer.

"This is Detective Borges, we need assistance at North Central 9826 and 23rd Street. We also need an ambulance and send down some well-known scientists. Don't ask any questions! Just do it! And be quick about it," yelled Detective Borges.

Eric read on the buzzer, and in case of being invaded of top secrets, press buzzer, and it would warn Doctor Corona. He looked around more and he saw that all that had happened was on camera. Not only that, but it was being sent live, by satellite to Doctor Corona.

Chapter XXI

Apprehension

"Look at this, You know that Doctor Corona knows that we are here. He might try to hurt Kimberly and Eric Junior. I have to get home!," said Eric.

"I will go with you, you need some back up," said Detective Borges.

"No, you need to see a doctor, you couldn't be much help to me the way you are. Just call in for help and send them to my address. I need the keys to your car," said Eric.

All right, here they are, please be careful and I hope the rest of your family is safe," said Detective Borges.

"Thanks," said Eric. And out the window he went.

He went down the alley to where the car was parked. He got in and started the car. He hoped that there was enough gas in the car because he had no time to stop. It was a long drive to get back onto the freeway and get to his home. He figured that if Doctor Corona was at the hospital, it would take him an hour, depending how fast he drove, maybe a little longer to find his house. That is if he had never been there before.

Eric went speeding through the traffic with the siren going. He put it on top of the car. He hoped that this would cut down his time a little.

He was going seventy to eighty miles per hour at times, racing into and out of traffic. He almost lost control of the car on a corner intersection, but managed to straighten out the tires.

Almost at his home street, he noticed the gas gage. He was really cutting it close. He pulled off of the freeway onto his street, 19th and Erie. He had about two blocks to go when the car coasted to a stop. Eric got out and checked his gun to see if he still had it. Then he ran like lightning to his house. He was panting when he came up on his house. He noticed a car parked across the street. He thought that was odd.

Eric ran up to the door. He was going to get the key out to open the door when.......it opened as he touched the key to the knob. He went inside carefully. There were no lights on inside. Maybe Kimberly went upstairs to bed early, but he knew better. He tripped over something, he almost fell, but he caught himself. He reached down to see if it was Kimberly......no it was furry, Roggow had been shot.

Eric headed for the nursery. No Eric Junior. He then headed upstairs. He didn't find Kimberly either. He ran down the stairs when he heard a scream.

"Kimberly!," he yelled, and ran out the back door. There was Doctor Corona holding Eric Junior and there was Kimberly lying on the ground with her head bleeding.

"So you found out our little secret, did you? Now you have ruined all my work and money that I was going to receive. You are going to pay dearly for this! I am going to take Eric Junior here for my new little experiment! You will never see him again, nor Tara. I have a self-destruct button in my car that as soon as I get inside I will push it! The whole building of Sanction B&F will be nothing but ashes! So throw down your gun," yelled Doctor Corona.

Eric knew that he had to do something. He held out his hand with the gun in it and picked up a brick with his other hand that was behind him. These were Kimberly's bricks that she had bought and piled up for one of her projects. Thank goodness that he could reach one without stooping. As soon as Doctor Corona's eyes were on the gun he dropped, he threw the rock hard at his head. Down went Doctor Corona and so did Eric Junior. Wailing and mad but unhurt, because he flew out of the doctor's arms into a sand pile, another project of Kimberly's.

Eric ran over to get Eric Junior, when he felt a sharp pain, in his left side. He fell and hit his head on a small corner of brick. Dazed, he could see cloudily through his eyes that Doctor Corona was taking Eric Junior around to the front of the house. He knew that he had to get the everlasting strength in his body to use, to get up and stop the doctor.

Eric got up, rock and rolly, went over behind himself and reached down to get the gun. He hung onto the house and went around to the front. He tried to get across the street to the doctor's car. He knew that he couldn't make it. The doctor saw him and was laughing, and was just about to push that button when......Eric took a deep breath......held as steady as he could......drew his gun......aimed......and fired directly into Doctor Corona's head.

But it was Eric then who fell to the ground, bleeding profusely now, then blanked out. When he came to, Kimberly was standing over him with Eric Junior, in her arms. They were all getting into the ambulance. He could see from the doors before they were closed, all the cop cars and the police around their house.

"Where are we going?," asked Eric.

"Would you believe to Mercy General?," said Kimberly.

Chapter XXII

Getting Closer To The End

Eric blanked out again, and hearing sirens in his dreams. They got him into the emergency ward and off to surgery. Kimberly and Eric Junior waited in the waiting room.

Eric was in surgery a couple of hours. He didn't wake up until the next morning. Kimberly was at his side, she had a bandage around her forehead. Also Detective Borges was there with her.

"Hi honey! How are you?," said Kimberly, and she kissed him on the head. "You gave us quite a scare when I woke up. Oh! By the way, nice shot!"

"Detective Borges, in Doctor Corona's car is a button, and it is a Saction B&F destruct button! Have your men take care of it! Do you have Tara out and the other babies?," asked Eric.

"We found the button, Doctor Corona's finger was just an inch away from it when you shot him. My men designated it already, so no problem," said Detective Borges. "As for Tara we have her and the other three babies downstairs. Being watched by honest doctors."

"I still don't understand why they dumped those babies? What was their reasoning?," asked Kimberly.

"Those babies were clones. They cloned them from when you were pregnant. Doctor Corona took a cell from your Tara without you knowing it. This was your first pregnancy, just like the other mothers of the other two. You never asked what the doctor was doing or about the tests. You just took his word for it. He was a doctor! People are supposed to trust their doctors, right?," said Detective Borges.

"Clones! We have more Tara's then?," asked Kimberly in disbelief.

"No, they only cloned one and she was at the dump. By the way, that was a neat idea Eric," said Detective Borges.

"What neat idea?," asked Kimberly.

"I put inside of the baby that they had dropped off at the dump, in her mouth, the word, unknown. I found a label machine in the closet and scissors and I cut it out and put this inside her mouth," said Eric.

"Why did they save the blood?," asked Eric.

"This was to make sure of the testing done at the so called Noitcnas, which they had to send back in a few days to Mercy General. See, the real babies, they didn't want to take any blood from them because it would slow down the project. Anyway, the blood from the clones, were the same, so who would ever have known," said Detective Borges.

"Also Kimberly, getting back to your question as to why they dumped those babies and maybe others is......what we found looking through all the data is this......Clones cannot be used because they have defects in their structure that shows up now or later. They didn't want to make a mistake on their project," said Detective Borges.

Chapter XXIII

Epilogue

"Can't you take us down to see Tara now? After all that we have been through! We need to see her and find out certain things that the doctors might tell us!," said Eric.

"Can a nurse watch Eric Junior for me?," asked Kimberly.

"I think that can be arranged and we might as well go down and get this done. I'll ring for someone to put you on a gurney and help you on the elevator. I want to advise both of you to be strong," said Detective Borges.

Detective Borges rang for an orderly and called the nurse. The orderly moved Eric gently onto the gurney. The nurse picked up Eric Junior and hugged him.

They all went down the hall to the elevator. Now Kimberly and Eric knew this way well. They both counted the floors down. The orderly moved Eric out of the elevator and Kimberly and the detective followed down the corridors to four and to six. They were told to go into room five.

The orderly moved Eric close by Tara. She had been moved out of the tub onto a small gurney and still had a respirator on her.

The doctor who was working on the babies wanted to be sure that this was Tara. He wanted to know if they had any solid proof since there were no fingerprints or footprints taken.

"Yes!, said Eric, open her small mouth and in between her lip and lower gum is something."

The doctor tenderly and carefully pried open the small mouth. To his amazement inside was part of a name, the name Shaw. Eric then told them that upstairs, in his wallet was the rest of his credit card.

"Is she still alive, then doctor?," asked Kimberly.

"Just for the meantime. She has been under dehydration and the drug they used on her gave her enough brain damage for a coma. I have run some tests on her brain and she isn't in a deep coma as yet. I want you to know, that if you had not saved her, they might have done those brain grafts on her without knowing that she could still feel the pain. That would have been a horrid way to die," said the doctor.

By now the tears were in Kimberly's eyes and Eric's too. They knew now that they had done the right thing. They also knew that she was really going to die soon.

"Can I hold her? I never have had a chance to hold her! It doesn't seem right if we can't hold her and let her know that we love her dearly before she is taken from us again!," said Kimberly sobbing.

The doctor readily agreed and told Kimberly to sit down in the chair. He has the detective help hold the respirator while he handed over precious innocent little Tara to her now-found loving mother.

Kimberly was still sobbing, but she took a couple of deep breaths and held and rocked her baby girl tenderly. The detective and the doctor pushed Eric on over to be with them. Then the doctor and the detective went out into the corridor and closed the door.

Eric took his arms and outstretched them as for as he could and touched each of his loves.

"Rock-A-Bye, Rock-A-Bye, Sweet Little Dear One, heaven had sent you for a short time. Rock-A-Bye, Rock-A-Bye, Sweet Little Dear one, you know that you are mine. Rock-A-Bye, Rock-A-Bye, Sweet Little Dear One, see you in heaven. Rock-A-Bye, Rock-A-Bye, Sweet Little Dear

One, remember that mommy and daddy love you forever," sang Kimberly.

She held her Tara close to her breasts, and little Tara died. They knew that she knew that she was loved, because she had a smile on her sweet little face when she died, smile of warm love!

About the Author

June Coover was born in Lexington, Nebraska. A mother of four grown children and seven grandchildren, June is a singer and songwriter. She had an opportunity to go to Nashville and she did two songs, and is hoping to get back there to finish two more. Writing has always been her dream, either in poems, songs or manuscripts. When her children were growing up she always made up songs and stories for them. Mrs. Coover enjoys life and the people around her. Her dad was the local blacksmith and was known for his tales. She believes that is where she inherited her writing talent.

www.ingramcontent.com/pod-product-compliance
Lightning Source LLC
Chambersburg PA
CBHW050407290526
45786CB00003B/1165